Heather Riches, a daughter of a miner, was born in Yorkshire and educated at Hemsworth Grammar School. She trained as a college lecturer at Huddersfield University, though most of her teaching was done in the South Yorkshire coalfields. Although interested in poetry from an early age, she did not start writing until later in life. Her writings reflect many of her experiences and the people she has encountered. She is married with two children and is now a grandmother of three.

For my husband, Roger John Riches

Heather Riches

VOYAGER

AUSTIN MACAULEY PUBLISHERS™

LONDON • CAMBRIDGE • NEW YORK • SHARJAH

Copyright © Heather Riches 2023

The right of Heather Riches to be identified as author of this work has been asserted by the author in accordance with sections 77 and 78 of the Copyright, Designs and Patents Act 1988.

All rights reserved. No part of this publication may be reproduced, stored in a retrieval system, or transmitted in any form or by any means, electronic, mechanical, photocopying, recording, or otherwise, without the prior permission of the publishers.

Any person who commits any unauthorised act in relation to this publication may be liable to criminal prosecution and civil claims for damages.

A CIP catalogue record for this title is available from the British Library.

ISBN 9781398499782 (Paperback)
ISBN 9781398499799 (ePub e-book)

www.austinmacauley.com

First Published 2023
Austin Macauley Publishers Ltd®
1 Canada Square
Canary Wharf
London
E14 5AA

Table of Contents

Lift Up Our Hearts To Gold

Giant mountains teeming with spoils of old.
They encircle homes and families in their fold.
All life is there to serve their master.
A prehistoric serf with gold to barter.

It glistens black and shiny below,
calling its servants to enter the show.
A watery dawn shows men ending their night of toil.
Hob nail boots clatter, snap tins clank, a smell of machinery and oil.

Blackened dusty faces, swinging lamps and head torches aloft.
They head in formation towards an oasis of home and soft.

A village listens for sounds of accident or mishap.
The mine controls their waiting and accepting.
Men know it can raise an ugly head, misfortune and trap.
Posthumous gains deliver only grief untold.
Lift up our hearts to the darkest gold.

Freedom For Me

Our house is all to me.
Walls, corners and fresh flowers on my sunny wooden table.
Everlasting, poignant and perfumed ministry.
I cry out to the overflowing memories.
They clasp my heart so fiercely.
A speaking, telling dynasty.

Here are all my waking thoughts.
My hopes and shielded times from where?
Happiness, challenges and ideas in the gilded air.
Do not lift a sombre brow; it needs no stamp or furrowed care.

Pretend you live life's niche in time.
My passing through will conclude as for all creatures alive.
For my love and home is freedom for me.

Wing of Dark

A flapping blackened state, all set to view a princely wake
Of pointed hat and billowing cloak
Of broom and wart and hideous croak.
Pretend the sky is twinkling light
With gorgon features set out bright.

A scene of bats and rats and toad
Silently disguise the velvet night and quietly detect a flight.
A flight seemingly awash with creatures of a sight
So horrible, they bring the fluttering dawn as a
Passenger of our heightened fright.

So shall we always breathe a ghastly sigh?
Constantly shall we preserve this annual withered eye.
Bring out all those silhouettes of cauldron, cat and why?
Sufficient at least it seems that Halloween becomes
A ghostly figment of our soporific dreams.

Clowns and Frowns

"Prepare yourselves today," the papers excitedly say.
Why should we expect to do that and in what way?
The ring resounds before us, clamour and mayhem abound.
The circus is a maelstrom of energy and sound.
Childhood rings aloud in older ears.
Memories seduce our waiting and sedentary fears.

A group of family clatter, holding ice creams,
Popcorn and reeling chatter await with gleam.
They have already dreamt the scene.
Bikes fall apart and faces painted in scream
Begin to speed around the saw-dusted circle.
Baggy trousers and giant shoes point gaily
And brightly to amuse.

Thrills and falls enchant the childish waves, who
Cry or laugh, interpreting each colourful save.
Buttonholes spray a front-seated crowd.
An instant recoil producing a howl of mercury sound.
Let it all go and wave it away.
Let clowns, not frowns, engage a tumultuous day.

Winter, Rose Red and Snowy White

A summer releases its hovering grasp.
The sun lowers its gleaming orb, a warm embrace
Of tentative fall, welcoming early winter's call.

The omens are good; they strike a note.
A leafy descent promotes a crackling golden earthly coat.
It is perfect for a reflected sheen.
Perfect for times colourful yet lean.

Obscurity sets the tone of creatures scurrying towards home.
What splendour this England of ours imparts,
With outward serenity and lively hearts.

Squirrels keep watchful eyes on battles won and lost.
No dialogue is apparent now.
They know the score and scorn a vow.
It's all for life as winter descends.
All are enemies; none are friends.

Pitch your song, bed low for the long night,
Winter, rose red and snowy white.

There's a Silence

Laughter and shouting are finished.
The house resounds silent and plain.
Childish voices, mute scrambling, no longer retained.
Hollow, encapsulated air fills memories, lifting all care.
Sounds of family and home enter a new refrain.

We were always remembered as many.
Thought as one and loved each other the same.
Generations askew, known lovingly in a time frame.
Never forgetting each in affection and true name.

Now the split is complete, new families emerge.
Paths of parental memory now diluted, remembered
From afar, dutifully saluted.
Different is life now, no requirement of response or licence.
There's a silence.

Amelia is Sleeping

A small figure is sleeping, oh such a delight
Maybe now we can all relax for the night.
A tiny nose showing from the edge of the cover.
A wisp of hair fluttering in cute repose,
Don't we just love her?

The ballpool is silent and forlorn.
Does she dream of its colours and give a sleepy yawn?
Let's creep to the bathroom and hurriedly clean teeth and face.
Only ten yards or so now to our own warm, snug place.

Just a minute, a light seems to be glowing.
A trip to the switch will present another delay.
Sweet sleep, how you do call me from so far away?
Resist any further peeping.
Amelia is sleeping.

"Two Times"

A small person, I should say
Will have an enormously satisfying day
Balloons and gifts with crackers and more.
Pretend the boxes are really only to store.

I presume his gifts are appropriate too
A book, a toy and maybe a silver-gilded shoe
Something new and exciting, curiously inviting
A two-year-old's view of two times anew.

His mummy and daddy caress this dear lad
His grandma and grandad approve and are glad
A bonus, of course, you have to admit
A family completed with happiness lit.

Remember your birthday, remember it well
The clatter and chatter of family swell
Small voices are calling now, surely you hear
A boy, a two-times boy in his third year.

Something isn't Always

You can hear something seething under the air.
Retracting quickly should someone appear.
A creature determined to leave its lair.
A condition creeping forwards, quickly and near.

Yesterday it remained unchecked, its progress kept at bay.
Something is not always connected to what we say.

We like to imagine our character is thoughtful and kind.
Connection seems seamless and always well timed.
Alas! Wait a while and shadows are back, and feeling blind.
I meant to relay my thoughts candid and whole.

Some people need a pathway and toll.
Please don't test my voice and expression as being too bold.
Something isn't always meant as it is told.

A Marriage for Lovers

A chime in their hearts which shimmers and is true,
Today, has a relevance proving presentment is due.
We think to the past and we begin to smile.
It's time to forego our singular mile.

Two together make possible a reaction that rings along where hearts converge.
Hold dear that sentiment and trustworthy surge;
We wish to consider our lives and imbue,
A cupid resolve to promise the years anew.

Remember the setting with flowers array,
Inviting the beating hearts to run astray.
Sweet sentiments on card and gift become yours for perpetual time,
Explicit in its surroundings from the utter divine.

A Boy for Keeps

An early morn, a babe is born.
He keeps all awake who are present there for his sake.
A tiny head, a silent thread to prove his life is lively and entire.
I am the first to see the blue-eyed boy and the signal to dawn that he will aspire.

Changes ahead which bring to scene a
Clattering of boots and a military dream.
We witness a growing young man,
Sharpness of stealth and keen of eye.
He rallies ahead but minds return to that bed.

Protect this young warrior from whatever is thrown.
He will always be fierce in our hearts now he is grown.

Better to be Back for Christmas

Waiting around, the Christmas tree now betrays an impatient sound.
Decorated and situated to promote the greatest treat,
Its tinsel turns and reflects any escaping gleam.
It colours and envelops the thoughts of all things it could possibly seem.
Everything is now prepared, all times and even lost repairs.
It does not matter how ticking clocks seem in reverse.
Christmas is its own universe.

Dinner is truly a wonderful feast.
It delivers a taste of many years before,
When all around the table were countable and not least.
Dishes of succulent meats and devourable sighs
Were piled to meet starving highs.
Now family tides will reside in their usual chairs,
To reflect their importance and guise,
No one questions the number or volume of courses taken.
An event as this is not to be mistaken.

But wait, have our memories slipped and abated.
This year will tell of missing laughs and exploding jokes.
Two Christmas crackers will occupy their boxed retreat—splendidly yoked.

Flushed faces, radiant and aware, remember a reason to take care.
History moves on but should not differently declare.
A stable scene with mother and child ever dictates our family's thoughts.
Better to be back for Christmas.

Every Brick of That Wall

End to end and wide and tall.
I need all the dawns that brim and fall.
What tales I will try to recall always finish at that wall.

The chapters of life are chipped and endlessly
Arranged, lined up and curiously assigned.
We test our memories against their tight
Formation, damage limitation.

Was an event the one which changed your life and happiness had begun?
Perhaps a character from the past created an eclipse of your sun.
You will need every brick of that wall until your chapters are over and done.

Remember your bricks and sigh.
That solid line will never lie.

Probably Not

We search our Earth for people past and push our boundaries over.
We are a passing host at most for life's meagre span.
Years are superficially and visibly crossed,
But where are the sights and sounds of our presence here? Are they lost?

Possible only to refer, photographs and films prefer.
We leave not another jot.
Our history reflects a cloud of making, not only our own we moan.
Shrouded in times and people who ride our lives as if they were their own.
Are we therefore chained down to accept our unrequited history is probably not.
We leave not another jot.

Red Rum

Whispering victories amidst clamour and shout,
He gallops his heart and soul to brush and wood, over and over.
Preserve this glorious creature and have no pretentious doubt.
His life is of brilliance and innumerable lives of worship.

A tidal morn begins his day, waves of mist, time and grey.
Man astride the muscle and bite.
Hooves of steadfastness and flight.
The sky controls his edge and sight.
His is a mercurial and precious crest of might.

True gentleman and pleaser of souls and true prescriber of many a dream.
Bring out your claim and tie your fortunes to this vivacious animal scene.
He will compete and perpetuate a legendary proposition,
A horse to feed the every scheme.

We'll see you there, red and starlight.
You'll take your place with precision and faith.
Green-carpeted rest and fading crowd bright.
Push hard and give our fate a twist.
Christened Rummy and bravery kissed.

A Gentleman of Time

To all families we must prime our light.
An era of humility, resounding and polite,
Now has left our world and permitted this night.
But consider it not as gentle or as bright.

A current of sadness must not pervade.
He brought children's laughter and all things
That are made from continuity, and most of all
Of a grade that none will surpass in our lifetime
Of achievement parade.

He wants none of our grief and none of our tears,
Push back all this sadness, unfold all the new years.
He cannot be forgotten as holly is green.
His aura still lingers and can always be gleaned.

With simple name and abounding pride.
A wife so solid, a permanence at his side.
Although he is now perfect and beyond our reach.
Consider whatever you have in mind is something within your own niche.

Grandchildren and children join in our thoughts for this day.
Ninety times years present a consuming display.
A display of goodness and fulfilment as well.
A story along the generations to tell.

I've Looked at Life From Both Sides Now

When I was young, life unsung.
Projects started with energy, conscience rife.
Successes, losses, studies of added strife.

It paid to slow and let life dictate.
It pulled and pushed into shape.
Shapes began to grey.
They only mattered for perhaps one day.

I rushed to seek youth and verve.
Fresh seasons leaving shadows on painted earth.
Remember what you tried to seek?
Every memory screamed, "Bleak!"

No one knew my innermost schemes.
Leaving behind my favourite dreams.
I no longer scrape and bow.
I've looked at life from both sides now.

Winter's Dawn

Winter's touch is reaching now; it quietens birds and stills the plough.
The sea wreaks havoc with might and foam.
Moonshine completes a scene of brine crescendo, a silvery moan.
Creatures rush to seek a retreat for home and rhyme.

Nature would plunder her earth, given land and time.
She commands and scythes her strength with no man's permission.
Her heart is God-given and needs not to seek remission.

Fruits of autumn seem heartless and small.
They supply our lives with hope and must spread to all.
What misery would abound and signify a missing of life's call?
Alas! One broken pause, one broken wing, one weakened pawn.
One sacrifice to winter's dawn.

You Can be Brightside

You think you can be nearside?
Don't speak offside.
I'm thinking you can communicate.
Try and walk on by.
I'll bring on rain to arrest any lie.

Just look my way—yesterday, today or any day.
Pick up the pace.
How fast can you race?
Ready now to judge this space?

So popular, so jocular.
My, oh my sunnyside.
Never stop cloud bashing and rainbow trashing.
The rain will subside.

Let me know.
Don't let them beat you down.
Be brightside, alongside.
Positive thoughts, cheery waves.
Forget dark side and dark caves.

Look topside; avoid landside.
You can be brightside.

Donkey Ride

"A donkey ride?" I hear you cry.
Roll up; prepare to be astride.
The ears are keen, revolving and bereft
Of all timely pride.

He is your complete superior.
Possess a momentum humble and slow.
He will trudge the sands of beach and time.
Did Jesus whisper his name in rhyme?

It's Bobby or Susan or Mickey or Flo.
Make a plan; cast aside your rage and go.
Give him a sign; he knows them well.
His divine rider prepared him for you and
Every other soul as well.

Tiger Day

Sonorous start though pale and tepid dawn.
A rapid evacuation of all things senseless, tasteless and forlorn.
I understand your beating heart, that today is
Of the tiger born, and things are arriving.

Nothing left and nothing sided in stark relief.
Seek my opinion, both bold and spare.
No wafting, amorphous thoughts in there.
Trust my judgement and regard my energy, nothing is trite.
Only remember that my tiger day is connected from night to night.

Navigate now from the following morn,
the Clouds of mistrust, posturing and resonant scorn.
"Another listless, shapeless day," I hear your voice already worn.

The Engine Fixer

A fragment of the pink and yellow dawn
Arises haltingly but never forlorn.
It signals to the worker inside that his day
Is now set apart, and so is his pride.
He must finish his breakfast and raise his heels.
No longer to be thinking of comfort and meals.

He collects his bike and commences his day,
Imparting a sigh, feeling feet of clay.
A wintry landscape awaits his comings and goings.
Never downcast, he has a cheery wave, always outgoing.
His neighbours relinquish a moment to notice his hesitant smile.
Thoughts now of labour and the rain-soaked mile.

Sandwiches packed for makeshift respites, to curtain the work, let in some light.
They are carefully chosen and prepared for this daily blight.
A little contrast to grind and sweat, a feeling of warmth to icy fingers and snow.
The engine fixer, or Harry as we know.

Light

A candle flickered dumbly, its light relieved my soul.
A waxy, organza glaze shimmering in a deep, dark,
Transcending, monotonous hole.

Are you afraid or unaware of truth and wanton faith?
Come and protect that light, its stream and vibrating transparent glow.
Capture it and restrain it within your own halo.

Light exists for all to test.
A heartening journey is interminable sometimes, but will reveal its need.
Persist your effort, release its contest, provide your best.
Triumph your darkness and take the lead.

A Rising Smile

A child I see along my paths away, showing a
Pattern of all things known and knowing.
Delight is heavy and consuming, squared off with vigour.
Fear has a very different figure.

Calm and loving days make a jaunty, Skippy blaze.
An excursion ahead perhaps, or gifts given now or in the past.
Words to praise are guaranteed to lift our souls and love to last forever.

The events stark and bold are written across the
Faces portrayed, though verbally untold.
Pretend a day of amusement tall, and note the resulting rise and fall
Apprehension overtaking joy makes its unknown timetabled wall.

A family possesses and kindles all reactions to all transactions.
Read the smiles to find the show that signs the atmosphere below.
Below the canvas fresh and bright, is it a rising
Smile or expression of sadness and fright?

Golden Horses

What will scare my senses?
Behind my thoughts, I commence my ride.
My journey here contained doubts and Signs, will the worries darken my day?
It leaves a trail of cold dismay.

I travelled towards the light, transcended by my fight to stay alive.
Persuading myself I will lose nothing,
But gain condition and conclusive concord.

The horses bring a fullness around my being.
A moment figured full and lavish, all-seeing.
The gold is shining and rich in an age of brilliance and glitter.

Why did I ever consider it a sham or fraud?
My golden horses heal all and celebrate the life I laud.

"Two's Retirement"

A double act, no more to stay.
They brought a scheme along its complicated way.
A pristine light guided their precarious flight.
Hole in one, what more satisfying and immense delight?

The years ascend and no more can we say.
Tomorrow, pretend; tomorrow is another day.
Cast aside now those Yorkshire-spent hours.
Time is now bereft of waking and sleeping towers.

So raise aloft this gallant twosome.
Give voice to all that divides their lives anew.
The scythe has cleaved, yeah split, their years and times and true.
Ride forth and christen two times two.

Greens and family schemes seem to clamour.
Sights and sounds of past resounding drama.
Release all this memory and record it well.
To change is to shed an age of fulfilment and pastoral knell.

Friends and colleagues, all fixtures and plans.
Remain a part of any travels along the length of any lands.
Take our encouragement, and remember us now
Proceed with another time, another show and take a bow.

A Rose of Gold

Posturing slightly awry,
Clouds scudding relentlessly across a customary and loving sky,
A newness rings a knell of change.
Prescribes a time of faltering range.

We test and ride the crest of life.
It has no scheme, no type nor sight.
Following blindly, we ascend the process we began.
Are we to stand alone, cometh the light
Of this dome creating our creed and home?

Understand and grasp the tiny footsteps clattering now.
You are not to wonder why or how.
Life is not yet samely as of old.
The wind was scattering and laughingly cold.
When from God's own garden dropped a rose of gold.

Silver Celebration

A start in love where hearts converge
Released a timeless and enormous urge
Could years apace produce a theme and
Progress towards this convivial scene?
Could love depart?
I think not, against this affectionate and willing plot.

Serene those skies, serene those ties,
Bequest the two with unequivocal guise
This silvery dawn on sadness and laughter
On family and children and waking hereafter.
Protect this style, brush mind and guile,
Separation completely revile.

We celebrate a spring of clamour
A summer of voiced and happy alarm.
Small voices of babies, small tides of chatter
Pretend no more that two is the way
A clutter of charm now rules the day.

Ring out the chimes,
Proceed with care, break out the wine and disturb the lair
It matters not that hurt lies there
He will not have his chance of air.

Silver upon silver, a story still to tell,
Confetti and veils, a distant peal of wedding bells.
Complete this task and prime your light
Guide love and power and precision of sight.

Future Space

It beckoned to me from a cast-iron place,
A sombre purpose propelled its one Preposterous grace.
We were walking towards our shallow and homely abode,
Nothing could present its true and revolutionary
Design upon this aching heart of mine.

Our winning and elusive offspring release this Timeless pace,
A child's eyes and a child's document of momentary haste
Did the length of life prepare us for our cannonball
Into levels of prime time, set mildly into a present cloud.

This relevant discussion amidst our family space
Another want, another question of light or perhaps solitary disgrace.
Can those hills and valleys evoke this flickering and distorted Haze?
Do we suspect our brilliance or not in the future phase?

Rosebud Perfection

A rosebud setting we have to declare
A man and woman present their vows and promises there
A church on the skyline, the sky azure-blue
A marriage for lovers, longing and loving and caring anew.

White silk and satin, flowers entwined
Her gown rustles and shimmers, reflects teardrops all round
The bridesmaids are perfect; they gaze and they smile
The strains of the choir resound mile upon mile.

All hush for their vows and thoughts at this time
Two people in love, their lives will now align,
Bringing settings for families, all anticipating their cue,
This wedding representing their hopes for gold-banded preview.

Confetti is thrown and voices raised to height
Floating veils gloriously hosted in a froth of delight
The couple is toasted with wine sweet and red
Music enchanting reflects their tentative tread.

Church bells sing out in their strident way.
Remember, remember this superlative display;
Consider it carefully; brandish your hearts on your sleeve.
Breakfast on memories, they have no cause to deceive.

Dark Horse

A worthy beast to bring me light
Of wiry mane and untold instincts of old,
She makes the world so calm a place,
I've learned to mock this rugged human race
With your equine grace I made my positive lines to always connect with thine.

Money plays no part in the customary yearnings of the heart;
Those faultless eyes and timeless sighs;
Those snorts and squeaks and deep disguise
to which I always place my mind,
You creature of brushing, silken thighs.

Ears that point to darkened sounds and cries,
Will you testify to all our lies, because we are all acquitted at the end;
Peace is something you ascend and there I could find you
Is man a burden to be found upon your wide and strengthened back,
Pursue and bring her back.

Imprisoned and astounded at the loveliness of you,
Your breed is only a caress of time,
You are watched and possibly detached from what we know of mine,
The smell and sweating skin will remind me of the hue of summer and,
Summertime can be relaxed as a gift.

As age began in a tempest of creature and man,
You have revealed my reasons for capturing prolonged and resonant disdain,
That flames flickers dumbly now she's gone.

www.ingramcontent.com/pod-product-compliance
Lightning Source LLC
Chambersburg PA
CBHW071257130726
47998CB00003B/1235